Write A Research Paper
in Six Easy Steps

D. Bryant Morris

ISBN 0-9653791-0-8
Copyright © 1997 by D. Bryant Morris
Made in the USA

Published in Chapel Hill, NC by
JenPrint Publications
121 S. Estes Drive, Suite 203-J
Chapel Hill, NC 27514
919-932-2413

Typesetting and printing by: The Chapel Hill Press

Table of Contents

Preface

This book is designed to be a how-to guide for the beginning writer. It provides step by step instructions on how to research, organize, write, and document a lengthy term paper or research project. It is not intended (or expected) that the writer will read through the entire book before beginning writing. Rather, the information contained in this work has been carefully divided into six self-contained units which the reader can easily access as he or she moves through different stages in the writing process.

To assist the reader in getting to the essential concerns of each unit, I have either highlighted or bulleted that information which seemed most useful for the beginning writer, with the hopes that this information could easily be retrieved at a future point in the writing process. Additionally, I have provided sample pages in the appendices of this work which should help the writer to quickly check his or her own pagination and formatting against a standardized form.

As a final note, I should caution that the "Documentation" section at the end of this booklet is not intended to replace an official style manual, which is essential for any major research project. On the contrary, it is my hope that this brief work will help to point young writers towards the resources they need to produce an intelligent and professional academic paper.

D. Bryant Morris

Blank

Step 1: Choosing a Topic

1. The Crucial First Step

The first step in writing a successful research paper is in many respects the most important one. Before you can write an informed, well-researched paper, you will need to make some basic decisions about your topic. Although the process of selecting a research topic often seems tedious and perfunctory, in reality, the decisions you will make in the earliest stages of your writing will have the greatest impact on your final composition. If, for example, you decide to take on a massive topic, such as global warming, in a 1500-2500 word essay, you will soon find yourself overwhelmed with information and unable to say anything meaningful about your topic. Likewise, if you commit yourself at an early stage to a research topic that either doesn't interest you or is insufficiently documented (that is, there isn't much written on the subject), you may very well find yourself afflicted with a severe case of writer's block, or what is worse, writer's boredom. Therefore, it is worth spending some time–even a considerable amount of time–reflecting up front on the topic you wish to write about. If it helps you to justify your investment, think of this time not so much as planning but as careful strategizing.

2. The Assignment

Begin with the assignment itself. If your instructor has assigned a topic to you, do not despair; in many ways, he or she has already done much of the preliminary work for you. Your job at this point is to carefully analyze the assignment given to you and make certain that you understand its requirements. If you already have a specific topic for your paper, you may want to skip to Section 3 which discusses "Interpreting Assignments" in more detail.

If your instructor has not provided you with a specific topic for your paper, or if he or she has only given you a list of possible research areas, then you will need to make some initial decisions on your own:

LENGTH AND SCOPE. The first such decision involves length and scope: how big and how broad should your research paper be? Most instructors will try to provide you with some guidance in this area.

Review the instructions given to you by your instructor or ask him or her personally to determine just how much you will need to write. Try not to think of this issue as a matter of word counts; your focus should not be on filling up a specified number of pages with black print, but on discovering the natural dimensions of your assignment.

Any topic that you choose to write about will have a predetermined amount of time and space necessary for its successful completion. In the case of global warming, for example, an intelligent and well-researched discussion of the many issues, controversies, and theories involved would require nothing short of a lengthy book. If, however, you choose a particular aspect of global warming, such as the negative impact of burning fossil fuels, then you will have narrowed the dimensions of your paper to something on the order of a detailed scientific report. An even more focused topic, such as "Fuel Emission Standards and Their Impact on the Environment," would finally put you in the category of a manageable research paper. Determining the length and scope of your paper before you begin writing is essential to producing a quality research project.

CLARITY AND FOCUS. This last point brings us to the second major decision you will need to make about your research topic, its specific focus. There is no more crucial stage in your writing process than this one. If your topic remains generalized and abstract, then your research will be less productive and your eventual writing will prove difficult and haphazard. By committing yourself at this early stage to a specific, concrete, narrowly focused subject matter, you will help to ensure that all of your future endeavors proceed smoothly. Avoid selecting a broad or sweeping topic under the mistaken notion that this will make it easier for you to "fill up" your assigned pages. In fact, such topics are often more difficult to research (you will be overwhelmed by information) and can be painful to write (you will spend more time squeezing them into unnatural dimensions then you would simply expanding upon them in full). A far better approach is to begin with the "length and scope" decision you arrived at above and ask yourself, "What could I reasonably write about in the dimensions I have set for my paper?" Your first thoughts, of course, will almost always be too general. That's OK! Because another important step in this process is to bring clarity to your selected topic.

Clarity is nothing more than specificity and concreteness. It involves taking a broad topic–global warming–and narrowing it down into something more manageable for the paper dimensions determined above. "What particular aspect of global warming could

3

I reasonably write about in a 1500-2500 word essay?" A precarious response to this question would be "The Causes of Global Warming." The causes in this case might be relatively few and concrete, but in order to explain them in any detail, that is, with any clarity, you will need far more than 2500 words. A more practical response, as we suggested above, might be: "Fuel Emission Standards and Their Impact on the Environment." This topic is still fairly broad, but at least it is concretely focused on one particular aspect of the global warming phenomenon. As you do further research, your topic will become clearer and more sharply focused. For the moment, at least, you will have made a good start toward producing a manageable research paper.

AUDIENCE. The final consideration to keep in mind as you begin selecting your research topic is audience. For whom is my paper written? My instructor? My classmates? Experts in the field? Amateurs? How much will I have to explain to my readers? How much can I assume my readers will know? These are all crucial questions for determining whether the topic you selected above will reasonably fit into the dimensions you have established for your paper. In the case of "Fuel Emission Standards and Their Impact on the Environment," for example, you will have a difficult time discussing your topic in any detail if you have to spend several pages explaining the background to the global warming crisis. If, however, your paper is for an environmental sciences course and you can assume a reasonable amount of familiarity with the subject, then you might very well write a focused paper in the required space.

Another crucial aspect of audience involves the tone and style of your paper. Knowing the intended reader(s) of your paper can be of great help in determining just how much research and detailed analysis your final product should contain. As you move into the planning and research stages of your paper, this knowledge will be especially valuable in helping you to budget your time and mental resources appropriately.

Having thus reviewed your paper assignment carefully, you should be able to make some tentative decisions regarding the future design of your paper:

- How long and how extensive will my paper be?

- What specific focus will my paper take and can it be clearly discussed according to my answer in #1?

- What is the audience for my paper and is it compatible with the answers in #1 and #2?

3. Interpreting Assignments.

If your instructor has assigned a research topic to you, or if he or she has provided you with a specific focus for your paper, then you will need to review his or her instructions carefully to determine just what the final product should contain. To do this, you will need to pay considerable attention to the specific language used in the assignment. For example, does the instructor ask you to explain, describe, compare, contrast, or evaluate a given topic? Each of these verbs means something subtly different for the writer and therefore will have a significant impact on the way in which you approach your final project.

An assignment that asks you to evaluate a specific topic, for example, is quite different than one which asks you simply to describe it. Description involves the straight forward reporting of objective facts; evaluation, as the word itself implies, involves making value judgments and offering evidence in support of your conclusions. The first step, therefore, in interpreting your research assignment is to circle or highlight any significant verbs. Once you have done this, you will then want to spend some time considering what each of these verbs means and what expectations they raise for your reader. Examples are provided below:

COMPARISON: explores similarities between two topics.

CONTRAST: explores differences between two topics.

DEFINITION: categorizes, classifies, or distinguishes a given topic.

DESCRIPTION: objective, detail-oriented presentation of the facts, conditions, or characteristics of a given topic.

EVALUATION: argument for the value, feasibility, or legitimacy of a given topic

EXPLANATION: demonstrates how or why a particular topic functions as it does.

INTERPRETATION: offers possible ways of understanding a given topic.

PROOF: provides evidence in support of a given topic or assertion.

REFUTATION: provides evidence against a given topic or assertion.

After looking at the specific language of the assignment, you will then need to consider two other related issues:

audience and length. Audience involves not just who the paper is addressed to (in this case usually the instructor) but also certain basic questions such as (1) how much knowledge or information can you assume your reader to possess, (2) will you need to provide extensive background information, (3) will you need to explain technical terms or jargon to your reader, and perhaps most importantly, (4) what will your reader be expecting from your paper based upon the assignment before you?

While you can never read the mind of your instructor to completely figure out what he or she wants out of a paper (indeed, such exercises are usually frustrating and futile), you can spend some time thinking about what the assignment asks you to do and how this fits in with the larger aims of the course. Try and ask yourself why the instructor has assigned this specific topic to you, worded in just this precise way, and what, if anything, this may have to do with your other activities in the class.

The second consideration is far more tangible in nature. The suggested length of your paper will usually be indicated on the assignment sheet itself. If it is not, you should consult your fellow classmates or the instructor to clarify this matter before you begin composing. Knowing how much and how extensive you will need to write is absolutely essential for planning the rest of your research paper.

Finally, you will need to take special note of any additional instructions provided on your assignment sheet. Usually these can provide you with some helpful clues as to what your instructor is looking for in your paper. If, for example, your assignment requires you to consult at least five outside sources, then you can be sure that your instructor is looking for a considerable amount of research; in this case, more than just summarizing a few choice articles.

If your assignment prohibits you from using first person voice ("I" or "me"), then your instructor is probably looking for a dispassionate, objective discussion of the facts involved. If your assignment makes a special point of emphasizing the importance of correct grammar or spelling, then obviously your instructor intends to read your paper very carefully, with an eye to prose style and mechanics. Of course, any specific instructions provided in the assignment sheet should be noted and followed exactly. No matter how much time and effort you put into the rest of your paper, you must follow basic instructions. As a helpful reminder, you may want to reread the actual assignment after each stage in the writing process. This will convince you of your own progress on the assignment and ensure that you do not make any careless errors in its completion.

4. Preliminary Research

Even after you have analyzed your assignment and given considerable attention to its requirements, you may still be uncertain about your topic. Specifically, will there be enough documented sources for me to complete this assignment, and even if there are, will I be able to comprehend and work with these sources easily? Essentially, questions such as these go to the issue of familiarity: how comfortable am I with the topic I have selected (or received) to write on?

An easy and advisable way to become familiar with your topic, or even just to test the waters, so to speak, is to visit the Reference Section of your local library and peruse some of its general reference works. Almost all professions or academic disciplines will have some kind of general encyclopedia, dictionary, or almanac to help you get a handle on your assignment. And since most modern college libraries use the Library of Congress cataloguing system, you will find any related reference works handily collected in the same general area. A good way to finish up the first stage in your writing process, and to build confidence for the upcoming stages, is to spend an afternoon in the library simply flipping through some of these works. As you do so, you may want to take note of the following concerns:

1. Are there any names, titles, or resources that stand out in the general rresearch about my topic? Usually an encyclopedia or dictionary will make reference to the leading experts or institutions in a given field. Take note of these as they will be helpful in the formal research stage of your project.

2. Are there any recurring terms or concepts that I do not understand? If you are having trouble comprehending even a basic discussion of your topic, then you may want to consider the feasibility of your proposed subject. Otherwise, take some time, while you are in front of a dictionary or encyclopedia, to look these terms/concepts up and become familiar with them early on. It will save you time and energy later on in the process.

3. Write down (or photocopy) any bibliographic information provided in the encyclopedia or diction-

ary entry. Many of these entries are written by people who are already experts in your selected field. It will be helpful to know which books, journals, newspapers, or scientific studies they believe are most valuable to understanding your topic.

If your library does not contain any specialized reference works in your area, you may want to consult a general interest encyclopedia. These books will provide you with an overview of your topic and may even be more helpful in supplying you with a pedestrian's knowledge of your proposed subject. However, remember that general reference works are not sufficient for a formal research project; you will need much more specialized information. Finally, you can consult the periodical section of the library and check out any leading magazines or journals in your area. While they will not provide you with an overview of your topic, they can be helpful in determining what some of the leading issues or problems are in your field. Indeed, they may even provide you with some fresh ideas about how to focus and clarify your preliminary topic.

5. Preparing For the Next Step

If you still feel uncertain or hesitant about your topic, you may want to discuss your preliminary ideas with your instructor. Keep in mind, however, that your project will also develop as time goes on and that this is only the first step in a very long and involved process. Also, do not be afraid to go back to the drawing board, particularly at this early stage. If you feel that a particular topic is not working out or that you are simply not prepared (for whatever reason) to write about it, that's OK.

It is better to come to this realization now rather than half way through the first draft of your paper. If you must scrap an idea altogether, do so, but you may also want to consider modifying or adapting your topic to meet your own needs, expectations, and interests. Once again, the more comfortable you are with a topic from the beginning, the better research project you will produce in the end.

Step 2: Research

1. An Evolving Project

No matter how much time you spend analyzing and refining your topic, you will soon reach the point when you simply must move on to the next stage of the process: formal research. In many respects, this is the only true way to get a handle on your research assignment. By reading widely in your subject area and by struggling to understand the arguments and interpretations put forth in your various sources, you will become far more familiar with your

topic than you ever at first imagined—or perhaps wanted. As with every stage in the writing process (but perhaps most importantly with this one) you cannot skimp on the hard work. Writing a research paper is only half the challenge; the other half lies in the careful preparation that goes into this stage of the project. You will simply have to resign yourself to spending a great many hours at the library (or at the photocopy machine). But if you budget your time wisely—so that you do not have to do all of the research at once—and if you follow the suggestions below as you move through your sources, you will find that it is not impossible to quickly and efficiently acquire the information you need to write your paper. More than any other stage in the writing process, formal research requires discipline and patience. With these virtues always in mind, you can easily master the scholarship in your selected field.

2. Strategic Researching

When you walk to your section of the library and survey the imposing wall of books waiting for your inspection, it is easy to get discouraged and begin choosing works at random, relying upon such subjective criteria as appearance, smell, or even type face. Occasionally, you will get lucky and come away with a few choice books, but more often than not, such haphazard research will cause more frustration later on in the writing process. Books that seemed, at first glance, to contain just the right material eventually yield only a few, cursory insights. Other works that seemed, based upon the flashy cover, to be the latest in contemporary research eventually prove to be a modern reprinting of a book written over thirty years ago. To avoid these kind of mistakes, and to help ensure that you make the most efficient use of your time, you can employ a method of strategic researching which will help to focus your efforts towards a specific goal.

FORMULATE A RESEARCH QUESTION: Before you go to the library, think back to your topic selection process and try to formulate a question, problem, or issue for you to focus on in your research. If, for example, you selected the topic of "Modernism and the Harlem Renaissance" as the subject for your research paper, you would want to express that issue in terms of a question or riddle that needed solving: "What was the effect of literary modernism on the Harlem Renaissance?" or "How did the Harlem Renaissance affect literary modernism?" or "How was the Harlem Renaissance part of the modernist movement?" etc. All of these questions address what is essentially the same issue, and all of them are worded broadly enough so as to allow the researcher flexibility and freedom when he or she goes to the library. Try to formulate a research question which will provide you with a specific goal or task–a concrete end for your many hours in the library–but also avoid an overly narrow question. Remember, at this stage in the game you are still exploring.

SURVEY THE MATERIAL: You should get a good idea right away about the appropriateness of your research question based upon the luck you have in finding quick references through the card catalogue or computer directory. If, for example, you went to your library terminal and typed in "HARLEM RENAISSANCE," you would find literally hundreds of works on the screen, covering everything from music to art to literature to urban history. If you then began limiting your searches based upon such criteria as "CAUSES," "PHILOSOPHICAL ANTECEDENTS," "LITERARY MOVEMENTS," etc., you would then be able to focus your efforts on more productive areas of interest. After all, you are not simply interested in the Harlem Renaissance, but more specifically, on its relationship to literary modernism. The best way to do this is to browse the system. Begin by looking through the subject headings under "HARLEM RENAIS-SANCE"; when you come to the sub-category "HARLEM RENAISSANCE AND LITERATURE," go inside and browse some more. Eventually you might even be lucky enough to come across a sub-sub-category such as "HAR-LEM RENAISSANCE AND LITERATURE–MODERN-ISM." At this point you could begin writing down (or printing out) any work that seemed relevant to you. If one work in particular seems appropriate, check its subject headings or related references to see how the computer system has categorized the material. A big part of navigating the library's vast amount of information is figuring out how exactly it is organized.

FORM A PRELIMINARY BIBLIOGRAPHY: The more you browse your library's card catalogue or computer system, the more promising works you will come across. Begin by jotting down any references you think might be important for future investigation, making sure to include the author, title, and library call number. If your library system allows you to make a hard copy of the computer screen, you can easily print out a list of several dozen works as a preliminary bibliography. Now you have a contained (say two dozen or so) list of works to consult on an initial basis. You may want to begin by checking out those books and reviewing them at your leisure; it is better to ease into the research process. The most important thing is that you now have a core group of works to launch your investigation. In subsequent weeks (and perhaps months) you will continually augment and build upon that list until you have a comprehensive bibliography of contemporary research.

BRANCH OUT: While you are working your way through this core group of works, you can vary your research habits by also looking into periodicals, newspapers, and abstracts. Most modern college libraries now contain computerized search engines which will allow you to survey current research at a computer terminal (rather than trudging through dusty stacks). Your local librarian can give you specific assistance on how to access and utilize this remarkable new research tool. Some programs even allow you to print out articles directly from your terminal, eliminating the need to hunt down and photocopy the original publications. As technology continues to expand in this area, search programs will undoubtedly become more specialized and comprehensive. Already many disciplines have tailor-made systems which access information specific to their field. Before you begin hunting at random, ask the reference librarian for help in determining which search programs are best for your needs. Once you have tapped into the right system, you can use the same method of selection as outline above for books: start with a core group of articles or stories and expand from there.

MAKE BIBLIOGRAPHIC *NOTE CARDS*: As you begin to review your core list of sources, you will quickly determine which works will be valuable (and which will not) in answering your research question. Remember to keep this question in mind as you move through large sources in particular. In the stream of interesting information which you will soon unleash, it is easy to forget the primary focus of your research project. Don't be afraid to explore, but also, don't forget what your main objectives are and how much time you have left before you need to begin writing. For some student writers, research is a black hole from which they never return!

When you land upon a source that you feel will be helpful to you in the writing of your paper, make a bibliographic note card recording all of its relevant publication information. This should include:

- author's complete name

- complete title

- publisher and place of publication

- year of publication

- number of pages

- volume number, edition, and title of publication (when appropriate)

Basically, your bibliographic note card should contain everything that you will need to complete a Works Cited list at the end of your paper. If you are uncertain about what this includes, you may want to browse the documentation section at the end of this work; it will help to clarify what you are looking for. It is vitally important that you record this information as you move through your sources; at the end of the assignment, when you are crunched for time, you will be thankful that you have this information easily at hand, and it will save you needless and wasteful return trips to the library. A sample bibliographic note card is printed below.

```
Sheldon Burke

Harlem Modernism

Bridgeport Press

New York, NY, 1989. 153 pp.
```

3. Research Note Cards

By now your "strategic researching" has provided you with a core group of materials from which you can begin assembling information for your paper. It is not enough simply to read through these materials carefully and perhaps jot down a few interesting points. You need to establish a method of systematically categorizing the information you encounter. The best means of doing this is to compose a series of research note cards which compartmentalize your findings in a convenient and easily accessible format. For each idea or quote or insight that you run across in your reading, make out a brief note card summarizing or paraphrasing (or in the case of a quote, exactly reproducing) this information for future use. Be certain that you limit yourself to one idea or quote per note card. Cramming too much onto one 3x5 space defeats the purpose of note cards, which is to allow you to access this information quickly and easily.

In addition, you will want to label each note card distinctly so that its content can be remembered at a later date; providing page numbers where the information can be found is also essential, as it will prevent you from having to search for this information in the documentation stage of your project. If you annotate your bibliographic note cards with a simple numerical system (1, 2, 3, 4, etc.) then you can use these numbers to indicate on your research note cards which sources you are summarizing, paraphrasing, or quoting. Think of these note cards as the building blocks from which the structure of your future paper will be constructed; the more time you devote to producing clear, informative building blocks, the easier your composing process will be. Whatever technique you develop in producing your own note cards, be sure to keep the following guidelines in mind:

- label all note cards for content.

- always include the page numbers from which your information is derived.

- always indicate which source you are using (hint: use numbers keyed to your bibliographic note cards).

- if you are quoting directly from the source, remember to copy the author's words directly as they appear in the original source and be certain to enclose them in quotation marks.

- if, as is frequently the case, your note cards are a mixture of summary, paraphrase and quotation, be sure to keep the author's words distinct from your own; always try to restate the information in your own words so that you do not inadvertently fall into the trap of plagiarism.

- compose your note cards legibly and completely; hasty penmanship and excessive abbreviation can obscure the meaning of your research.

- limit yourself to one idea or quote per note card.

A sample research note card is printed below for your reference. Standard 3x5 ruled index cards work best for this project: you will be tempted to cram too much information onto larger cards, and you will need the ruled lines to help keep your research legible.

> Definition of Modernism   1
>
> "An international movement in the arts brought about by the social and psychological upheavals of World War I and lasting well into the mid-twentieth century."

4. Preparing For the Next Step

There is no predetermined amount of time which you should devote to the research stage of your project. How much information you should assemble before you begin writing will be determined in large part by the nature of the assignment itself. However, try to avoid the common mistake (and strong temptation) to begin moving to the organization and composing stages of your project before you have thoroughly surveyed your assembled sources. You will undoubtedly discover new insights, ideas, and directions for your paper as you take stock of the research already done on your topic. If you find making note cards tedious, you can try to vary your research patterns by spending part of your time in the library and part of it recording your research notes.

The ultimate factor in determining whether or not you have done enough research for your paper will be the research question itself. If you feel that you now have more than enough information to adequately answer the question, then you are ready to move on. If you are unsure about your readiness, then you should review your current note cards and consider what additional information would be necessary to complete this task. Any nagging doubts or questions that you may have are probably best addressed at this stage in the writing process, when the material is still fresh in your mind. It will be harder to return to your sources when you are in the middle of your first draft. Of course, you will always have some issues or aspects of your topic that will remain unresolved; that is part of the allure of research. Try not to get bogged down in covering every single detail. Continually review the goals you set for yourself with the research question and evaluate your progress in the library according to this criteria. In a sense, it is the game plan you will use to successfully execute your "strategic research."

Step 3: Pre-writing

1. Shaping Information

Now that you have efficiently and systematically assembled the information for your research paper, you will need to shape this information into a logical and coherent pattern. The first step in this process will be to settle upon a tentative thesis statement. This will commit you early on to a specific and identifiable purpose for your paper. Determining the purpose of your paper is absolutely essential for writing a good research paper: since much information presumably already exists on your topic, you need to carve out for yourself a unique reason for writing this paper. What is it that my discussion aims to do, and how will it be different from the discussions which have come before it? Answering these difficult questions is the primary focus of the next stage in your research project: prewriting.

2. Tentative Thesis Statement

A thesis statement is basically a promise that you make with the reader: "I promise to prove, explain, discuss, interpret, compare, contrast, or evaluate the following topics for you in the following paper." Of course, no one words their thesis statement in precisely this way, but, essentially, that is what they are doing–making a commitment to the reader about what he or she can expect from the following essay, article, or research paper. Thinking of the thesis statement in this way–as a promissory statement–will help you to evaluate, at each stage of the writing process, just how well you are keeping to your stated objectives. Time and again, you should ask yourself: "Am I fulfilling the promise I made with the reader?"

To do this, of course, you will first have to formulate your promissory or thesis statement in a way that you can keep. It will not do you any good to make grand claims in your introduction that you know your research simply will not support. Similarly, you should not try to mislead your reader, promising one thing and then delivering quite another. Rather, it is best to formulate a thesis statement whose expectations you are confident you can meet. You may want to start by looking back over your research question. Usually the thesis statement for your paper will be the answer to that question. If, for example, you started with the research question "Why did the United States drop the atomic bomb on Japan?" then presumably the thesis statement for your paper would try to answer that question, presenting one or perhaps several different reasons for President Truman's decision.

In formulating your tentative thesis statement (it will be revised later), you should try to come up with a promissory sentence that fully commits you to a specific argument or interpretation. Simply saying "There were many different reasons for President Truman's decision to drop the atomic bomb on Japan" is not enough; such a sentence is a cowardly thesis statement, involving very little commitment on the part of the writer. The reader has no idea what to expect from such a statement because it in fact promises very little. Consider, however, the level of commitment involved in a thesis statement such as "President Truman's decision to drop the atomic bomb on Japan was motivated primarily by a desire to establish American military dominance in the post-World

24

War II era." Bold, specific, and even a bit controversial, this kind of promissory statement puts a lot more on the line. The reader of this sentence will have a very clear idea about what to expect from the writer's paper.

As you formulate an answer to your research question, and thereby begin crafting the tentative outline of your thesis statement, try to devise the most engaging and specific response possible. Of course, your answer should be grounded in the actual research you have done for the project (avoid overstating your argument), but also try to come up with a dramatic presentation of your ideas. Again, if you think of the thesis statement as a commitment or promise to the reader, then you will be well on your way to success.

3. Arranging Your Note Cards

Armed with your thesis statement, you now must begin marshaling the information your have retrieved to make your argument for you; you have made a promise–a commitment–and now you must keep it. The only way to do this is simply to dive in: spread your research note cards out in front of you on the floor and begin sorting them according to common themes. One stack of cards, for example, might involve Soviet efforts to develop its own nuclear technology. Another stack might deal with casualty estimates for a land invasion of Japan. Yet another might deal with the political pressures confronting President Harry Truman. Whatever your subject matter, you should find it fairly easy to begin grouping your note cards along related themes or concepts. After all, the research you have done was not haphazard; it presumably sought to answer the research question posed at the start. As you work through your cards, try to consider

25

how the information you collected best works to answer that question. As you arrange (and undoubtedly rearrange) your research note cards, you will begin to discover new connections in your work, and hopefully, a logical pattern will emerge for how to structure your argument.

Let's say, for example, that you sorted your research note cards into three distinct piles:

1. Soviet efforts to develop its own nuclear technology.

2. Political pressures on the U.S. president.

3. Military logistics and/or options for ending the war.

Already you can begin to see a logical pattern developing for the organization of your paper. Following the lead of your three major groups, you might envision a research paper with a traditional tripartite (three section) structure. In the first section, you could discuss outside pressures from the Soviet Union, specifically, the threat of an impending Soviet nuclear capabilities. In the second section, you might discuss the internal pressures on President Harry Truman, specifically, the need to end the war quickly and decisively, that is, with America on top. Finally, you could end the paper by discussing the various military options available to the president, explaining how the decision to drop the bomb on Japan satisfied both the outside and internal pressures outlined above. In this way, you would begin to construct an effective response to the question first posed in your research: "Why did the United States drop the atomic bomb on Japan?"

Of course, now that you have a basic structure for your paper (and be aware that you may have as many as five or six different piles in your first sorting) you will need to further classify your information. Begin by arranging your initial groups in a preliminary sequence. Starting with the first pile, sort the note cards in that group into smaller subdivisions. Due this for each of your initial piles of cards and take stock of your arrangement. Don't be afraid to experiment at this stage in the process! Take advantage of the flexibility afforded you by your note cards and modify your arrangement repeatedly, continually trying out new approaches. Remember, these are the "building blocks" for your paper and this is the fun part, the one where your get to play architect.

Once you have cobbled your research into a rough outline, take a moment to consider whether any section of your paper seems decidedly weak. Do you need more information on the Soviet nuclear program? Does your stack of cards on "Military Options" seem rather thin? If so, then now is the time to go back to the library to fill in the holes. As the saying goes, you want all your cards in place before you begin drafting a final thesis statement and formal outline.

4. Final Thesis Statement and Formal Outline

Now that you more or less know how the information in your paper will be arranged, you can put together a final, comprehensive thesis statement and follow it up with a formal outline summarizing the sorting you have just done. If, after looking over your note cards, you feel that you can better express the promise you intend to keep in your paper, then you will need to modify your tentative thesis statement. Most of the time, this modification will involve some minor clarification of information or narrowing of scope. You may find that you have more research then you can possibly ever use. If so, then decide what aspect of your collected information you wish to emphasize. Don't be afraid to remove note cards or even whole sections that don't fit well with your thesis statement; indeed, some excision of information is probably advisable, since you will almost certainly have an oddball quote or irrelevant summary somewhere in your notes. Sculpt the information that you have until it conforms roughly to the commitment you wish to make in this paper, then formalize that commitment by putting it in writing. This will be your final thesis statement–the contractual agreement for the rest of your paper.

In the example we have been working with, you want to modify your tentative thesis statement ever so slightly. You started off with the sentence:

> "President Truman's decision to drop the atomic bomb on Japan was motivated primarily by a desire to establish American military dominance in the post-World War II era."

Your revised thesis statement, based upon the outline mentioned above, might read something like this:

> Because of strong political pressures at home and abroad, President Truman sought to establish American military dominance in the post World War II era by unleashing the atomic bomb on Japan.

28

Here you have made a promise to your reader that you know you can keep. The mention of external and internal political pressures easily signals to your reader the major divisions of your paper, and the deft reasoning– "to establish American military dominance in the post-World War II era"–makes it clear how you will interpret the president's controversial actions. All things considered, it is a solid thesis statement.

Now to the outline. The format that you use to sketch in your outline is less important than the actual fact of getting your ideas onto paper. You can use words, phrases, even whole sentences if you like. The most important thing is that you write down the organizational scheme you have plotted on your bedroom floor. Of course, if you are one of those writers who likes to have everything planned out very carefully before you begin writing, by all means, draw up a formal outline complete with Roman numerals and complex organizational schemes. Some people feel more comfortable with only a loose outline. Still others find it easier to "block in" their ideas by reproducing their note card headings in abbreviated form. Whatever your personal style, be sure that your outline is thorough enough so that you can reproduce the organizational decisions you have already made; no need to do the work twice!

Once you have produced this written outline of your note cards–the blueprint, so to speak, of your research paper–you should fasten it in a visible location in front of your computer or typewriter. This will allow you to easily keep track of your progress while writing and ensure that you do not stray from your original plan. Remember, you have already made a commitment to your reader, and now you must follow through.

Step 4: Writing

1. The Well-Prepared Writer

There is no special trick to writing a research paper; the same principles of clear, elegant, unadorned prose apply equally to longer and shorter works of composition. The only difference between a research paper and an essay, then, is scope and complexity: the final draft that you produce for your research project will be far more involved than a simple argumentative essay. It will require you to tie together several major subject areas or lines of argument, and it will demand that you maintain the standards of good writing over a longer and more taxing period of time. In other words, it will require the qualities of both foresight and perseverance. At all times keep your eyes on the prize. If you remain focused on the final objectives of your paper, and if you proceed at a careful and even pace, you will find the writing of your paper much less arduous then you imagined at first. After all, you have already done a significant amount of work on your project. You have carefully selected your topic, patiently collected the necessary information, and systematically organized your materials. The only thing left is to translate that prep work into simple, unadorned English. The guidelines below should help you as you begin fashioning your project.

2. Writing As A Process

Writing is a process, and a process is something that unfolds over time. As you begin work on the first draft of your paper, try not to get too hung up on ironing out every detail of your composition. There will be plenty of time to revise and rework later. At this stage in the project, the most important thing for you to do is to begin shaping your ideas into a rough argument. Though the temptation to stop and continually revise your writing will be strong, it will be more productive now for you simply to plow through the assignment. Once you have fleshed out the entire project, you can go back and make some informed decisions about what needs to be revised.

3. Introductions and Conclusions

The introduction and conclusion are obviously two of the most important sections of your paper. In them, you will both lay out the argument for your entire paper (i.e., introduce your thesis statement) and draw together the various strands of your argument (i.e., synthesize the major points of your paper). In a research paper, which tends to be longer than most college writing assignments, these two sections are particularly important because they help to orient and then reorient your reader to the main thrust of your argument. In a sense, they are the bookends of your research project–the solid supports which hold the rest of your paper in place. Therefore, special attention should be given to these sections. Often even a well-written, well-researched paper will be marked down because of a seemingly weak introduction and conclusion. For better or for worse, it is these two sections which leave the greatest impression on your reader's mind.

In the first draft of your paper, you should not worry too much about sculpting a perfect introduction. Some writers even feel more comfortable writing their introduction after they have composed the main body of their paper. This way they will have a clearer idea about what it is that they must introduce. This can be especially effective when writing longer papers that will necessarily develop as they are composed. If you do decide to write your introduction up front (some writers feel that this helps to orient them to the material), do not be concerned if it takes you anywhere from 20 to 40 minutes to compose only a few paragraphs. The slow pace of your writing is a healthy sign that you are meticulously gathering your ideas into a focused introduction.

Whenever you eventually decide to write your introduction, keep in mind that the primary function of this section of the paper is to introduce your thesis statement. It is not intended simply to be a catchy or dramatic way of leading into your research. Rather, the introduction should provide the reader with some background or context essential for understanding the paper's main points.

Many writers choose to make the thesis statement the last (or next to last) sentence in the introduction; in this way, all the information presented in the introduction appears to build up to the central argument of your paper. This has led to the infamous "upside down triangle" paradigm whereby writers are told to start with a purposely broad opening sentence and then narrow their insights until they have arrived at the thesis statement.

In reality, there are many different ways to structure an introduction, all of them far more interesting than the hackneyed upside-down triangle approach. As you craft your own introductory paragraph, you may want to consider the following options:

a. Begin With a Quotation.

> "Kafka," says the poet W.H. Auden, "is the
> author nearest to bearing the same relationship
> to our age as Dante, Shakespeare, and Goethe
> bore to theirs."

The rest of the paragraph could then be an explanation
of this quote with the writer's remarks leading up to
some central interpretation or argument about the importance of Kafka's works to the modern world.

b. Begin With A Rhetorical Question.

> Who has been the most influential writer of the
> twentieth century? According to many critics, it is
> the German Jewish novelist Franz Kafka.

The rest of the paragraph would then be a justification
of this answer, with the writer's remarks leading up to
some central argument about the importance of Kafka's
works to the modern world.

c. Begin With a Controversial Opinion.

> Franz Kafka was undoubtedly the most influen-
> tial writer of the twentieth century, far more influ-
> ential than either Joyce, Eliot, or Proust.

Obviously the rest of the paragraph would need to be a
justification or defense of this claim, with the writer's remarks leading up to some central argument about the
importance of Kafka's works to the modern world.

d. Begin With a Contradistinction.

Although many of Kafka's works are obscure and incomplete, they seem to speak most forcefully about the condition of modern man. Here the distinction between Kafka's bewildering style and his literary importance are brought together to highlight some particular quality in his writing. It may be that it is this very style which accounts for Kafka's importance to the modern world, and so the writer has decided to draw attention to this point through the use of irony.

e. Begin With a Comparison or Contrast.

Unlike many twentieth century writers, such as Joyce or Proust, Kafka saw very few of his works published in his lifetime. As with "contradistinction," the writer will use comparison and contrast to highlight some particular aspect of his topic, in this case, Franz Kafka's unusual desire not to have his works published. Obviously the writer will need to relate this point to some central argument about the importance of Kafka's works to the modern world.

No matter how you decide to introduce your introduction, you must be certain that the main focus of this paragraph is to prepare the reader for the paper which is to follow. A beautifully written, intellectually captivating introduction is no good unless it sets up the main argument of your composition. Indeed, an overly grandiose or clever introduction can often doom a paper because it raises certain expectations which the content of the paper simply cannot meet. Therefore, you should try to strike a balance in your opening paragraph: catch the reader's attention and let him or her know what is at stake in your writing, but avoid sounding pompous or showy. The easiest and most honest way to do this is simply to tell your reader why you think your topic is important, and presumably, since you have already invested so much time in the project, you do think that it is important.

Conclusions are another matter altogether. Unlike an introduction, the main aim of your closing paragraph(s) should be to sum up, tie together, or otherwise restate the main threads of your argument. In this case, the standard model for how to write a conclusion is the right side up triangle, beginning with a specific point and ending with some sweeping statement of cosmic significance.

Once again, however, other models are available. You may wish to wrap up your discussion of a particular topic by bringing out some especially astute quotation which you have been saving till the end. Bringing in a well-known authority at the conclusion of your paper can help to give your own ideas more credence. Similarly, you might end your paper with some kind of forecast or prediction: what you are essentially saying here is "My topic is important because it will have such and such an effect on the future."

Another option would be to try to connect your topic or argument with some larger issue or concern. "What I have been discussing here is really part of a much larger issue, etc." or "The argument I have presented here has much broader implications, etc." Still another approach, and by far the most popular one, is a summary of the paper's main points. This can be particularly effective in a longer paper where the reader might very well miss the full scope of your argument. Here you remind your reader of each of the important sections of your paper, being careful to tie them in with some larger, unfolding conclusion which you are working towards.

Ideally, a review of the main points of an argument will lead up to the thesis statement, which is THE main point of the argument. Again, use whatever method works best. One word of caution, however: avoid introducing substantially new material into the conclusion of your paper. This is not the place to bring in new ideas but to sum up old ones. If you use any of the methods outlined above, your conclusion will sound fresh enough without any imported information.

4. Integrating Information

The body of your paper will largely consist of the information you have collected in the research stage of your project. In order to translate this information into a well-written research paper, however, you will need to integrate it into the body of your text. It is not enough simply to throw in a few quotes here and there with the hopes of proving your point. Just as the information for your paper was collected strategically, so too must it be developed and deployed strategically. The guidelines below will help you to do this and to ensure that the final product reads smoothly and intelligently.

4.1. Introducing Information

Each time that you use research information in your paper, either in quoted or paraphrased form, you must introduce this information in the body of your paper. By so doing, you prepare you reader for the material which is to follow and help to establish a critical context for understanding this information. In the following paragraph, for example, the writer simply interjects a scholarly quote without any sort of explanation or introduction:

> Any comparison of the Romantic movement within Russia to that of other European nations must begin with this basic point of departure: the Russian experience during the Romantic period differed from that of other great European nations because "it was during the Romantic period that the Russian nation developed its own national literary heritage."

Now consider how this paragraph is strengthened by the addition of an introductory phrase for the quotation:

> Any comparison of the Romantic movement within Russia to that of other European nations must begin with this basic point of departure: the Russian experience during the Romantic period differed from that of other great European nations because, in the words of cultural historian Max Rubin, "it was during the Romantic period that the Russian nation developed its own national literary heritage."

Here not only is the quoted material better represented as someone else's words and ideas, but also, the authority of the source, in this case a renowned cultural historian, is brought in to strengthen the credibility of the writer. Here it is clear that the writer is excerpting Rubin's own words because he feels that these words somehow support the argument or interpretation which he himself is trying to make. By using such introductory words and phrases you will not only produce a better written paper, you will formulate a more credible sounding argument. To help you in this regard, a list of possible introductory phrases is printed below:

- "as Rubin explains/ suggests/ notes/ argues/ believes/ contends. . ."

- "according to Max Rubin. . ."

- "in the words of Max Rubin. . ."

- "Rubin makes a similar point when he states/ argues/ observes. . ."

- "this view is reinforced by the judgment of Max Rubin . . ."

Just about any appropriately worded introduction will do. The most important thing to keep in mind is that all your research material must be attributed. Simply putting a page number or foot note reference is not enough. You must first explain why you are quoting the material and why you consider it an authority.

4.2. Using Quotations

In addition to introducing and attributing all of your research information you must also be sure that you are representing this information accurately. The basic rule of thumb for quoting from outside sources is this: whenever you quote from another writer's material, you must represent that material as authentically and honestly as you possibly can. Changing the meaning of an author's work by excerpting only selected words or phrases or by using such words and phrases without documentation is strictly prohibited. It amounts to plagiarism and can get you into serious trouble with your school authorities. At the same time, one needn't be reluctant to quote freely from outside sources. Indeed, using regular quotations to strengthen the claims you are making in your paper is absolutely essential to writing a successful research paper. To aid you in the use of such quotations, we have included the following guidelines:

1. Never use a direct quotation without some sort of introductory phrase explaining its origin and significance.

2. Never use another author's words or phrases without both quotation marks and some sort of formal documentation (e.g., footnotes).

3. Always reproduce another author's words or phrases exactly as they appear in the original source; if you have to make changes, be sure to acknowledge those changes through the use of brackets and/or ellipses (see below).

This last guideline will prove particularly important to you as you become more confident in using outside material. Before long, you will find yourself wanting to incorporate a phrase or passage which simply doesn't fit with the syntactical flow of your own paper. In such instances, it may be appropriate to introduce certain minor alterations to the original source, changing, for example, the verb tense or pronoun references to make them more consistent with your own writing. In the following paragraph, for example, the verb tense shifts uneasily between the explanatory and quoted material:

> In many ways, the differences between these two men embodied the coming rift between proponents of Westernization and those who wished to see Russian society develop its native store of Slavic culture. According to Rubin, "Karamzín has represented the convinced westerner who traveled extensively throughout Germany, France, Switzerland and England and who read many of the European literatures in their original language."

Now consider the slightly amended form:

> In many ways, the differences between these two men embodied the coming rift between proponents of Westernization and those who wished to see Russian society develop its native store of Slavic culture. According to Rubin, "Karamzín [represented] the convinced westerner who traveled extensively throughout Germany, France, Switzerland and England and who read many of the European literatures in their original language."

If you find it necessary to amend an original source for clarity or readability, you should always acknowledge your changes by placing them inside of [brackets]. Of course, any changes which you introduce should be of a minor, grammatical variety. Using brackets to alter the original sense or meaning of a quotation is not acceptable.

Another common emendation which writers frequently make involves the length of quoted material. Very often, for reasons of readability or economy, a writer will omit certain sections of an original source through the use of ellipses (. . .). As with brackets, ellipses should not be used to alter the sense or meaning of a passage, but rather, to bring out its most salient or relevant points. Consider the examples which follow below:

ORIGINAL:

> "The events surrounding the political uprising of 1825, in other words, helped to reinforce the ideological importance of literature (and really all such cultural-intellectual endeavors as they were recognized by the local intelligentsia) as a monitor of the historical destiny of the Russian nation. Poetry and artistic expression came to be seen as a vehicle for political and social renewal and thus the birth of Civic or Decembrist Romanticism."

REVISED:

> "The events surrounding the political uprising of 1825, in other words, helped to reinforce the ideological importance of literature . . . as a monitor of the historical destiny of the Russian nation. Poetry and artistic expression came to be seen as a vehicle for political and social renewal and thus the birth of Civic or Decembrist Romanticism."

As a general rule, three spaced dots (. . .) are used to indicate the omission of certain words and phrases; four spaced dots (. . . .) are used to indicate the omission of an entire sentence. You do not need to use ellipses at the beginning of a quotation.

Longer quotations (i.e., anything over four lines long) must be set off from the body of the text using a ten space indentation. These indented passages do not require quotation marks and should be singled spaced to further distinguish them from the body of your paper. See the example below:

According to Rubin, European romanticism helped to generate a Russian national literature:

> Thus we arrive at the strange paradox whereby a felt need for Russian self-sufficiency was assuaged by a philosophical and cultural ideology imported from Europe, in particular Germany. Romantic idealism, borrowed from the philosophical writings of Hegel and Schelling, allowed Russian nationalists, and even cultural isolationists such as the Slavophiles, to articulate their own country's desire for self-definition and discovery. (Rubin: 45)

One final suggestion with regards to quoted material. Try not to end a paragraph or paper section with a long quote; always add a sentence or two of explanation and analysis to help wrap-up your discussion of the issues. Paragraphs that end with a long, unexplained quote often sound incomplete in meaning and leave your reader craving for some sort of commentary.

4.3. Documenting Information

As you write the first draft of your paper, be sure to document (insert page references) for every piece of information which you refer to or directly quote in your argument. The final section of this manual provides more specific guidance with regards to documenting sources. For the moment at least, it is important to keep track of your reference material as you use it in the paper. Having to go back at the end of your assignment and reconstruct this information will prove time consuming and personally frustrating. If you do not yet know how you will document your research paper, you can simply place the author's name and any page references inside parentheses at the appropriate points in the paper (Rubin: 218). These will serve as markers for you when it comes to the final draft.

5. Interpreting Information

Beyond simply the mechanics of introducing and documenting reference material, there is also the issue of how often and to what degree you should rely upon quotes, paraphrases, and general summaries. As you begin to compose the first draft of your research paper, try to avoid the common misunderstanding that you must use every piece of information collected in the research stage of your project. Although you will want to put this information to "good use," you must remember that your primary objective here is to prove your thesis (i.e., answer your research question) and not necessarily to show off how well you can retrieve books and articles from the library. Again, the key term here is strategy. You must have a game plan for how you intend to use those valuable sources. Toward this end, it will be helpful here to review some general guidelines concerning the interpretation of source materials.

a. Never add quotes or paraphrases to take up space, but rather, to reinforce some point or interpretation you wish to make. Thinking of your reference material not as filler but as building blocks in a sound, persuasive argument will help you decide when and where to utilize such material.

b. Use direct quotations when you feel that the author's exact words help to make his or her point more concretely; use paraphrases when you need to summarize or restate an involved idea or discussion in a few choice phrases. Quoting bland material can seriously weakened the force of your argument as can needlessly restating a dramatic quote in trite, abstract language. When deciding how to represent source material, think strategically.

c. In addition to introducing (attributing) all source material, you should also try to give some spin or interpretation to the authorities you are quoting and/or paraphrasing. If you refer to a specific passage from a book or article, try to explain to the reader how that passage, and the points it makes, helps to reinforce your own argument. If an author says something provocative, explain why it is provocative. If the author makes some kind of implicit value-judgment, try to point that out to the reader. Finally, if there is some particular aspect of style or rhetoric that needs decoding, be sure to provide this for your audience. Remember, they will not all be as familiar with these sources as you are. Similarly, if you are re-stating the words or ideas of another author, try to do so in a way that brings out some of the issues discussed above. The more you tell your reader what is at stake in the argument your are presenting, and its various pieces of evidence, the more persuasive and readable your paper will be.

d. Avoid simply stringing long passages of quotes together with little or none of your own words interspersed between. Though this is a research paper, the majority of the writing should be your own. Relying upon others to write your paper for you can be a tempting but ultimately disastrous policy. The more you make the materials your own, through interpretation and analysis, the more coherent your paper will sound.

6. Preparing For the Next Step

The first draft of your paper will necessarily be an incomplete and unsatisfactory one. No matter how much planning and organizational work you do, you will always discover the main body of your ideas as you write. And that is how it should be. Once you have completed a first draft of the entire paper, you will want to proceed quickly to the next stage: revision. In this stage, you will refine your ideas and polish your writing. For the moment, it is important that you complete the enormous task of translating your general ideas into concrete language.

Step 5: Revising

1. Revising For Content

Once you have completed the first draft of your paper, you will want to begin revising and rewriting for both content and style. Concentrate first of all on content: after you have modified the actual framework of your argument you can always go back and fine tune the writing. And besides, it won't do you any good to craft a stylistically sophisticated paper if the ideas and insights aren't up to snuff.

After you have completed the first draft of the assignment, review your research question, tentative thesis statement, and preliminary outline. This will refresh your memory about what you intended to address in your paper. As you begin to read back through your first draft, stop yourself after each paragraph and ask: "How does the previous block of information help me to prove, explain, or qualify my thesis statement?" If you cannot immediately answer this question, odds are that neither can your reader. As you begin to interrogate your own argument in this way, you will quickly discover which sections of the paper needs revision (usually clarification and revision) and which can be left as they are. Occasionally you will run upon a section of the paper which, upon reflection, does not seem particularly relevant to your topic (it is easy to get distracted into interesting side issues); if this is the case, you will either need to find a way to tie that information into the main thrust of your argument, or you will need to delete it altogether. Don't be afraid to get rid of needless information, but also, don't be reluctant to explain things to your reader in full. It is always better to be more explicit than obscure.

The following list of questions will help you in the initial revision of your paper:

1. What is the thesis statement of my paper? Under-line or circle this statement.

2. Does the introduction of my paper provide neces-sary background material?

3. Does the introduction of my paper contain my the-sis statement?

4. How are the different divisions/sections of my pa-per distinguished from one another? Underline or circle any transitional passages between sec-tions.

5. Does each section of my paper progress in a logical order? What are the justifications for presenting my material in this exact order?

6. Does any section of my paper needlessly restate or repeat previous information?

7. Does any section of my paper seem out of propor-tion with the rest of the paper? Too long? Too short? Too detailed? Too abstract? etc.

8. What is the strongest section of my paper? What is the weakest?

9. Does each section of my paper use quotes or paraphrases regularly? Are there any long passages without outside references? Are there any passages with too many quotes (i.e., almost none of your own writing).

10. Are there any uninterpreted or unexplained quotes in my paper? Paraphrases?

11. Does the conclusion of my paper restate my thesis or summarize my main points?

12. Does the conclusion of my paper explain or reinforce the significance of my argument?

13. Does the first draft of my paper roughly follow the plan of my preliminary outline? Where does it depart and why?

14. Does this paper successfully answer the question I posed for myself in the research stage of my assignment?

2. Revising For Readablility

After revising your paper for content, you will now have the second draft of your project. By this point, you should have carefully examined each section of your assignment to ensure that it effectively contributes to the main argument of your paper. If whole sections need to be revised or expanded, this should be done before you move to the second stage of revision: revising for readability.

Readability is similar to content but slightly different: it involves not so much the structure and organization of your paper (which should have been corrected by now) as the ease with which you express and communicate your ideas. Essentially, this involves looking at your paper from a reader's perspective: how will my paper sound to someone not as familiar with my subject? Even if you can assume a significant amount of understanding on the reader's part (say a professor), you will still need to make sure that you are expressing all of your ideas clearly and forcefully. It is easy, in an assignment of this length, to become deceptively intimate with your material; after working with your sources for so long, you may forget that not everyone, perhaps not even your instructor, will understand the material as well as you do. Therefore, it is worth taking the time to read the second draft of your paper aloud. By experiencing your own writing in this way, you will begin to get an imperfect sense for how your work will sound and feel to others. As you move through the second draft of your paper, you may want to keep the following questions in mind.

1. Are there any sections of my paper which are difficult or cumbersome to read? If so, you can bet that your reader will stumble over them.

2. Do any sections of my paper sound jargony, colloquial, non-professional, or needlessly argumentative? If so, revise for proper tone.

3. Are there any sentences which seem too long (i.e., you have trouble saying them in one breath)?

4. Are there any sentences which seem too short (i.e., the rhythm of your prose sounds halting or choppy)?

5. Do any sections of my paper sound abstract or verbose? Do I have trouble understanding any section of my paper?

6. Are there clear, smooth transitions between each section of my paper? Does the paper seem to make a "sharp turn" at any point in my argument?

7. Does any section of my paper sound repetitive or wordy?

8. Does any section of my paper sound rushed or underdeveloped?

9. Do my introduction and conclusion dramatically focus and sum up my main argument?

10. Do I overuse any words or expressions? Are there any clichés or unexplained technical terms in my paper?

3. Revising For Style and Grammar

Now that you have revised your paper for content and readability, you are ready to make the final changes for the finished product. Since you have already reviewed the structure and sound of your paper, all that will be left for you to revise at this point are the mechanics of your writing. This will involve two primary aspects: grammar and style. For rather obvious reasons, you will need to ensure that every word in your paper is properly spelled and every sentence properly constructed. An intelligent–even brilliant–argument can look silly when sullied by a few careless errors. If you are using a computer or word processor, you can begin your final revision

51

with a spell check; this will catch a lot of the obvious typos.

Next, you will need to go through each section of your paper very carefully, making sure that little details such as punctuation, capitalization, and usage are properly addressed. To help keep your mind fresh, try to proofread in small blocks of time; reading through your entire paper in one sitting will make your eyes weary and less observant. Finally, you will need to pay some attention to the style of your paper: does each paragraph have a clear topic sentence? do I avoid using the passive voice? are my pronoun references clear and unambiguous? etc. Once again, to aid you in this stage of the revision process, you may want to refer to the list of questions below which cover most grammatical and stylistic issues of concern:

1. Are there any "surface errors" in spelling, punctuation, capitalization, or proper usage?

2. Are there any sentence fragments or run-ons?

3. Are there any split infinitives or dangling prepositions?

4. Are there any ambiguous pronoun references?

5. Do I properly use its & it's; there, their, & they're?

6. Does each paragraph have a clear topic sentence?

7. Are there any long paragraphs which need to be divided up?

8. Are there any short paragraphs which need to be combined?

9. Are there any passive sentences which could easily be made active?

10. Are there any being verbs (is, was, are, were, etc.) which could be made more active?

11. If first person ("I" or "me") is used in the paper, is this appropriate (see instructor)?

12. Are all titles of books, articles, newspapers, journals, and films underlined/italicized?

13. Are all abbreviations used consistently and correctly?

14. Are all quotes over four lines long separated and indented?

15. Are all quotes and paraphrases properly documented (see next section)?

After you have carefully poured over your paper, making whatever corrections or rewrites seem necessary, it will be helpful to do a final spell check to catch any typos that may have crept in during revision. As a final safeguard, you should read the assignment guidelines again thoroughly to make certain that you have met all of the necessary requirements. Any special instructions specified by your professor should be double-checked for compliance.

4. Preparing For the Next Step

When you have produced a final, clean copy of your paper, you will need to make certain that all of your sources are properly documented. It is important that you have your project in its final form before beginning documentation, since any changes you make in the revision process might easily affect the Works Cited or end notes section of your paper. Removing just a single quote from the body of your paper, for example, can change the numbering of all subsequent references. Similarly, you need to have the pagination of your paper in its fixed form before you can begin putting together a table of contents or index.

Step 6: Documentation and Formatting

1. Finishing Touches

The final touches to your research paper will involve documenting your sources and formatting your paper to meet the professional standards of your academic discipline. Both are absolutely essential for producing a quality research project. For rather obvious reasons, each source or piece of evidence which you refer to in your paper must be properly cited, that is, full credit must be given to the source through the use of a bibliographic record.

A standard bibliographic record will contain the author's name, the title of the source material, a brief publication history, and page numbers for the specific information referred to in your quote or paraphrase. Failure to provide this information constitutes plagiarism and can seriously jeopardize the credibility of your research project. Because you will have already kept a careful record of the page numbers and bibliographic information for each of your sources (remember your bibliographic and research note cards), you will have no trouble easily incorporating this information into the body of your final draft. To assist you in this regard, a brief overview of the four major methods of citation are provided below under the heading "Documenting Sources."

When you have completed the documentation stage of your paper, you will have completed all but the final step in your research project: formatting your manuscript to meet the professional standards of your specific academic discipline. In plain English, this simply means adjusting the layout and organization of your paper to follow the prescribed rules regarding use of page numbers, paper margins, section headings, title pages, or any other related matters of appearance and formatting. To assist you in this regard, a sample page for each of the major sections of your paper is provided in the appendices to this booklet. Of course, any specific instructions from your instructor or academic organization will always supersede these suggested guidelines.

2. Documenting Sources

As a writer, you will want to use an official style manual to insure that your work is documented thoroughly and accurately. Using a consistent method of citation, you will be able to communicate the content and quality of your research as well as to suggest possible sources for further study. In the United States, there are four major style manuals: (1) the Modern Language Association's Handbook for Writers of Research Papers, (2) Kate Turabian's Manual for Writers of Term Papers, (3) the American Psychological Association's Publication Manual, and (4) The Chicago Manual of Style.

Before you begin documenting your paper, you will need to clarify with your instructor which method of citation he or she prefers. Many instructors have very specific expectations with regards to the documentation of your paper, so it will be wise to follow their instructions carefully. *DO NOT SIMPLY MAKE UP A CITATION METHOD OF YOUR OWN.* This is both unprofessional and confusing for your reader. As the overview below will suggest, there are a variety of different approaches available to the writer, each capable of meeting the diverse needs of your paper. Whatever citation method you select, be sure to follow its specific guidelines without fail; any digression from the prescribed method defeats the purpose of a uniform citation code and may cause confusion for your reader.

Parenthetical Documentation:

Parenthetical documentation provides an abbreviated version of the full bibliographic record within the text itself, thereby allowing the reader to survey this information without scanning to the bottom of the page. A full list of bibliographic sources then appears at the conclusion of the work providing a more detailed account of publication history. In the MLA and Turabian style manuals, parenthetical information includes the author's name and the page number(s) where the information can be found. In other guides, parenthetical information includes the author's name and the date of the publication. In all three cases, if the author's name is mentioned in the text itself, there is no need to repeat it in the parentheses. Thus, correct parenthetical documentation can be presented in some of the following:

MLA and Turabian Style Manuals:

- Farrell provides a different explanation for the Gaelic Revival (234-245).

- The Gaelic Revival has been explained differently (Farrell 234-245).

APA Style Manual

- Farrell (1982) provides a different explanation for the Gaelic Revival.

- The Gaelic Revival has been explained differently (Farrell, 1982).

<u>Parenthetical Citations:</u>

Seven of the most common bibliographic entries for the parenthetical system of documentation appear below; these would be included in the "Works Cited" or "References" section of your paper (see appendices):

BOOK–SINGLE AUTHOR:

Farrell, J.P. <u>Modern Irish History</u>. New York: Albatross Books, 1982.

BOOK–MULTIPLE AUTHORS:

Manning, Tom and Joan Richardson. <u>Ecological Disaster in the Soviet Union</u>. New York: Holden Books, 1995.

ANTHOLOGY:

Witherspoon, Daniel, ed. The Oxbridge Anthology of English Literature. New York: Oxbridge Press, 1984.

WORK IN AN ANTHOLOGY:

Swift, Jonathan. *A Tale of a Tub. The Oxbridge Anthology of English Literature.* Ed. Daniel Witherspoon. New York: Oxbridge Press, 1984. 1024-1146.

ARTICLE IN A MAGAZINE OR JOURNAL:

Maddox, James. "The Betrayal of the GOP" *National Partisan* 7 June 1996: 32-35.

NEWSPAPER ARTICLE:

Morrison, Edgar. "Tobacco Lobbyists Blowing Smoke" *The News and Chronicler* 1 June 1993, final ed.: 1A.

DISSERTATION:

O'Gorman, Kevin "Artist as Priest in James Joyce's *Ulysses*." Diss. Western Carolina University, 1996.

ARTICLE IN AN ENCYCLOPEDIA:

Kopek, Jan. "Prague." *The Encyclopedia Anglia:* 1992 ed.

Footnote Documentation

Footnote documentation provides a full bibliographic record on the same page in which the source is cited, always at the bottom of the page and identified by a raised Arabic numeral. There is no "Works Cited" section in this style of documentation, although a separate bibliography may appear at the end of the text. Seven of the most common bibliographic entries for the footnote system of documentation appear below.

WITHIN THE TEXT:

Farrell provides a different explanation for the Gaelic Revival (446-456).1 In his recent history of modern Ireland.

AT THE BOTTOM OF THE PAGE, separated by a Short (20 Space) Rule Line, such as —————

[1] J.P. Farrell. *Modern Irish History* (New York: Albatross Books, 1982), 234-245.

BOOK–SINGLE AUTHOR:

[1] J.P. Farrell, *Modern Irish History* (New York: Albatross Books, 1982), 234-245.

BOOK–MULTIPLE AUTHORS:

[2] Tom Manning and Joan Richardson. *Ecological Disaster in the Soviet Union* (New York: Holden Books, 1995), 67-69.

ANTHOLOGY:

[3] Daniel Witherspoon, ed., vol. 3, *The Oxbridge Anthology of English Literature* (New York: Oxbridge Press, 1984),1457-1458.

WORK IN AN ANTHOLOGY:

[4] *The Tale of a Tub*, ed. Daniel Witherspoon, vol. 2, *The Oxbridge Anthology of English Literature* (New York: Oxbridge Press, 1984), 1024-1146.

ARTICLE IN A MAGAZINE OR JOURNAL:

[5] James Maddox, "The Betrayal of the GOP," *National Partisan*, 23 (1996): 32-35.

NEWSPAPER ARTICLE:

[6] Edgar Morrison, "Tobacco Lobbyists Blowing Smoke," *The News and Chronicler*, 1 June 1993, 1A.

DISSERTATION:

[7] Kevin O'Gorman, "Artist as Priest in James Joyce's *Ulysses*" (M.A. thesis, University of North Carolina-Chapel Hill, 1996), 15.

ARTICLE IN AN ENCYCLOPEDIA:

[8] "Prague," *Encyclopedia Anglia*, 15th ed.

In the appendices, you will find the first page of a sample research paper, followed by a works cited list. Refer to these examples throughout your study to help understand the format of your assignment.

A research paper, by its definition, is a long and intellectually involved process. Unlike the much shorter descriptive or argumentative essay, it requires going beyond the bounds of ones own expertise and experiences in order to synthesize those ideas with the broader range of human knowledge. In short, it requires you to enter into a dialogue with the professional community of scholars. They are often researchers who spend a lifetime wrestling with the kinds of issues that you may only devote a few intense months of study.

The completion of a research project such as the one outlined in this book is a major accomplishment and a reason for justifiable pride. By producing a well re-searched, well written and well argued piece of scholar-ship, you have made a contribution to the progress of human understanding. All too often, students look upon such an assignment as a chore, a monstrous task that must be laboriously and systematically dispensed with in order to pass a class or complete a degree. Thinking of your research paper as a contribution to the larger community of scholars and readers who comprise your field can help give your assignment new meaning and purpose. By completing your research assignment, you will have experienced one of the greatest satisfac-tions of an educational career: the knowledge that you have completed your task and that you have made a posi-tive contribution.

Appendix A: Title Page

<pre>
                    Morris 1
              (1 inch margin from top)

Daniel B. Morris
Professor Smith
English 22
15 July 1996

                 Re-creating the Self:
    Personal Identity in Defoe's Moll Flanders

As one of the earliest novels in the Eng-
lish literary tradition (xi), Moll Flan-
ders might be read as an extended
meditation on the mutability and imperma-
nence of the human self. Over the course
of this detailed autobiographical work,
the narrator alters her persona some thir-
teen times, each of them representing a
subtle shift in economic, religious, and
sexual affiliations. To be certain, there
is no such character as 'Moll Flanders"
to be found anywhere within the novel;
rather, the central figure of this story
is continually undergoing a process of re-
formulation and unpredictable develop-
ment. Indeed, almost every
</pre>

(1 inch margin from bottom)

Appendix B: Works Cited List

(1 inch margin from top)

WORKS CITED

Defoe, Daniel. *Moll Flanders*. New
York: Oxbridge Press, 1985.

Forster, E.M. *Aspects of the Novel*.
New York: Court Bryant Johnson, Inc.,
1927.

Barnet, Tad. *The Oxbridge Guide to
English Literature*. New York:Oxbridge
Press, 1996

(1 inch margin from bottom)

Index